DUCKS DUCKS

To the Students
at Verdi E. S.
May the ducks
bring you joy
& the stars their
wishes! Love
Theodocia
Swecker

Written and Illustrated by

Theodocia Swecker

To my daughter, Mackenzie,
who inspired this story and
to our dog, Doc, who now
runs among the stars.

The paintings were done in watercolor on
140 lb. Arches cold pressed paper.
The text type is Benguiat Frisky.
Designed by Pam Zunini

Printed in Hong Kong
by South China Printing Co. (1988) Ltd.

FIRST IMPRESSION
ISBN 0-9666537-0-X

"Library of Congress Catalog Card Number:" 98-93607

Summary: In the cold of the Nevada mountains
white ducks help an old mountain lion find
a warm spot to sleep.

DUCKS PUB.
155 McCoy Street
Winnemucca, NV 89445

A Note from the Author

When winter comes to Nevada, the wild ducks migrate south and leave behind the Peking ducks who are too heavy to fly. These white ducks are sometimes raised by ranchers to swim in the cattle's watering hole. They keep the water from freezing over. It's not uncommon to see white ducks living in a grove of Aspen trees, sharing the land with mountain lions and other wild animals.

During the winter white ducks, as well as other native wildlife, must find warm places to bed down.

"**QUACK, QUACK,**" said the ducks,

wishing they had a warm spot to sleep.

"**BURRRR**," said the old mountain lion.

"I'm tired of being cold."

" Quack,

Quack,   Quack,

Quack, "

said the ducks.

" We want to sleep with YOU!"

"GRRRRRRR,"

said the old mountain lion." I'm going to sleep in my tree."

" Qu **Quack,** Qu **Quack,** Qu **Quack,"**

said the ducks." We'll go too. We'll join you."

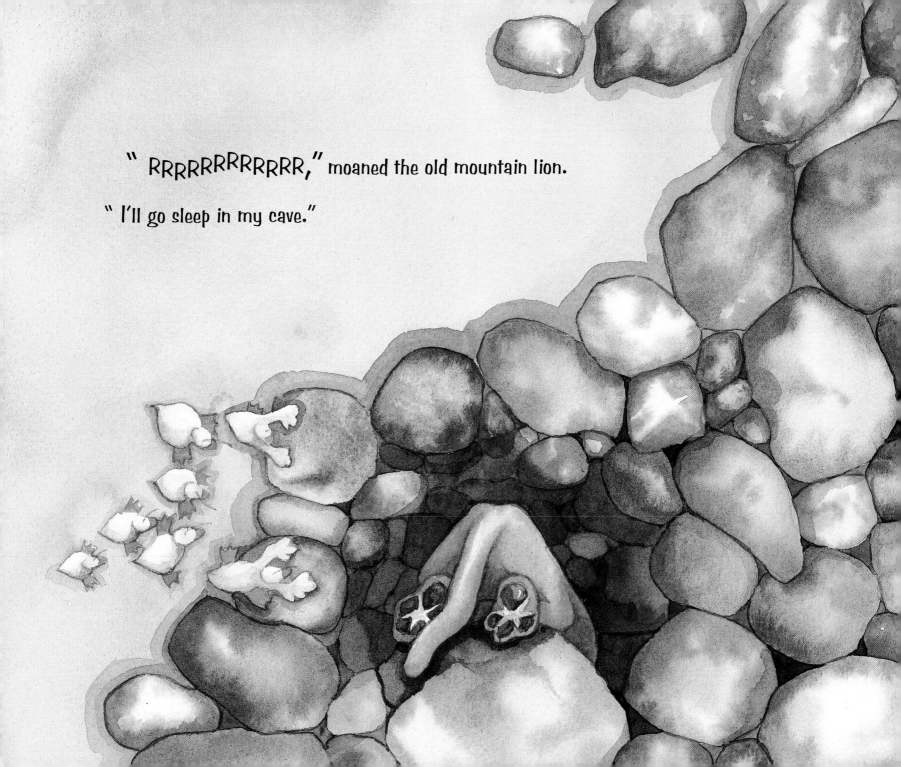

" RRRRRRRRRRR," moaned the old mountain lion.

" I'll go sleep in my cave."

"**Uggggg**," groaned the old mountain lion.

"I'll go sleep on my mountain."

" quack, quack, QUACK, quack, quack, QUACK,"

said the ducks.

" That is an imPECKable place."

"SSShhheeeze," whined the

old mountain lion." I have no more sleeping spots."

" QUAAAAAAAACK. QUAAAAAAAAACK.

Come with us," said the ducks.

" QUACK! QUACK!
QUACK! QUACK!"
said the ducks." Sleep here!"

"Quaaaack, quaaaaaack," said the ducks.